© Zeynel Abidin

Elif Shafak is an award-winning British-Turkish novelist and the most widely read female author in Turkey. She has published seventeen books, eleven of which are novels. Her work has been translated into fifty languages. Her latest novel *10 Minutes 38 Seconds in This Strange World* was shortlisted for the Booker Prize and RSL Ondaatje Prize, and chosen as Blackwell's Book of the Year. Shafak holds a PhD in political science and she has taught at various universities in Turkey, the US and the UK, including St Anne's College, Oxford University, where she is an honorary fellow.

An advocate for women's rights, LGBT rights and freedom of speech, Shafak is an inspiring public speaker and twice a TED Global speaker. Shafak contributes to major publications around the world and she was awarded the medal of Chevalier de l'Ordre des Arts et des Lettres and is a Fellow of the Royal Society of Literature. In 2017 she was chosen by Politico as one of the twelve people 'who will give you a much needed lift of the heart'. Shafak has judged numerous literary prizes, chaired the Wellcome Prize and is presently judging the Orwell Prize. *www.elifshafak.com*

ALSO BY ELIF SHAFAK

HOW TO STAY SANE IN AN AGE OF DIVISION

ELIF SHAFAK

First published in Great Britain in 2020 by
Profile Books Ltd
29 Cloth Fair
London
ECIA 7JQ

www.profilebooks.com

Published in association with Wellcome Collection
Wellcome Collection
183 Euston Road
London NWI 2BE
www.wellcomecollection.org

5 7 9 10 8 6

Printed and bound in Great Britain by CPI Group (UK) Ltd, Croydon CR0 4YY

The moral right of the author has been asserted.

A CIP catalogue record for this book is available from the British Library.

ISBN 978 1 78816 572 3
eISBN 978 1 78283 728 2

IT WAS MY FIRST DAY in Istanbul, a breezy evening in September, many moons ago now. Young, and aspiring to become a writer, I had moved to the city without knowing anyone, following an instinct I could neither identify nor betray, and rented a tiny flat in one of its most cramped, chaotic and cosmopolitan quarters, close to Taksim Square. From the teahouse across the narrow street I could hear the roll of backgammon dice over wooden board, the cries of seagulls darting and diving to snatch a sandwich from the hand of an unsuspecting passerby. But now it was late into the night, and the teahouse was closed, the seagulls roosting on rooftops. There were no curtains or blinds on my windows and bathed in the pale light from a street lamp outside I sat on a cardboard box full of books and papers, listening to the sounds of the unsleeping city. I must have dozed off for I woke up to the clamour of shouting.

I looked out and there she was, walking down the street, limping furiously as she carried a shoe with a broken heel in one hand while doggedly keeping on the other shoe. Clad in a short skirt, a silk blouse. A tall transgender woman. I knew the neighbourhood was home to sexual minorities, this being one of the relatively liberal quarters of the city, although their lives and livelihoods were constantly overshadowed by social prejudice and systematic discrimination. With no other job opportunities available, many within the local transgender community were either sex workers walking the streets or employed in the bars, clubs and taverns that formed Istanbul's night-time economy. In areas a stone's throw away undergoing rapid gentrification they had been driven out by police brutality but there was still a considerable close knit and proud community on my street, namely the *Street of Cauldron Makers*.

As she passed under my window, I could hear her talking to herself, and I was able to catch some of the words in her soliloquy. Someone – perhaps a lover, perhaps the whole city – had treated her badly, unfairly. She was sad, but more than that she was angry.

It started to rain, and the drops quickened,
   drip drip drip.
A single heel echoed against the cobble-
   stones, tap tap tap.

I watched her until she turned the corner at the end of the street. I had never before seen a woman so visibly broken, and yet stubbornly carrying on. I felt guilty for not opening the window and talking to her, asking if she was all right. I also felt ashamed because my first reaction had been to retreat into the safety of my flat as though I feared her melancholy might be contagious. It remained etched in my brain, the similarities and the contrasts. Her loneliness, which I sensed was no different from my loneliness. Yet my timidity as opposed to her boldness. She had had enough of Istanbul, I hadn't even begun to discover it. But more importantly, she was a strong fighter, I was just an observer.

Many years have passed since then. I no longer live in Istanbul. But today, as I sit at my desk in London to write about our polarised and troubled world, I find myself remembering that moment, remembering her, and I find myself thinking about anger and loneliness and hurt.

*

The pandemic. As the coronavirus swept round the globe killing hundreds of thousands, putting millions out of work and shattering life as we knew it, board signs appeared randomly in public parks across London. 'When all this is over, how do you want the world to be different?' the signs asked. What *all this* meant was not explicit in the question; passersby were expected to work out for themselves what it implied – this sudden disruption of our daily routine, this sense of being caught in the swell of uncertainty and the fear of what is to come, this major global health crisis with long-term economic, social and possibly political consequences, this tunnel that we, as humanity, must go through without any easy guesses as to how or when it would end or whether another outbreak of a viral disease might happen again in the near future.

The boards were deliberately left blank so that underneath the question people could write their own answers, and many had. Of all the comments scribbled hastily there, one in particular stayed with me. Somebody had etched out in bold letters, 'I want to be heard.'

When all this is over I want to live in a different world where I can be heard.

It was a personal cry. But, in many ways, it felt like a collective cry too.

'Who, if I cried out, would hear me among the angels' hierarchies?' asked the poet and novelist Rainer Maria Rilke in his *Duino Elegies*, written and published in the earlier part of the twentieth century. It was a different time back then. Today, in the twenty-first century, in a deeply divided and increasingly tangled world, craving dignity and equality, overwhelmed by the speed of change and the acceleration of technology, our shared feeling is, 'Who, if I cried out, would hear me among the humans' hierarchies?'

People who have much to say, a distinctive story to tell, often do not do so because they fear their words will fall on deaf ears. They feel excluded from political power and, to a large extent, from political and civic participation.

Even if they were to shout their grievances from the rooftops of Westminster – or Brussels or Washington or New Delhi – they doubt it would have the slightest impact on public policy. Not only management and authority, power and wealth, but also data and knowledge are increasingly concentrated in the hands of a few – and a growing number of citizens feel left out, not so much forgotten as never noticed in the first place. As their disillusionment deepens, so does distrust even in the most basic institutions. More than half of the people living in democracies today say their voice is 'never' or 'rarely' heard.* If this is the general mood in the relatively democratic countries, imagine how much higher that percentage would be in authoritarian regimes where there is no transparency and a single narrative is imposed from above, stifling any form of dissent. Added together, that is a lot of voiceless people. And the biggest irony is that all this is happening at

---

* Survey conducted by Dalia Research, Alliance of Democracies and Rasmussen Global, 2018.

a time when we as humans – regardless of race, gender, religion, class or ethnicity – are supposed to be more connected and empathetic and free than ever before, with far more opportunities at our disposal to express ourselves than our grandparents could have dreamed of, given the proliferation of both digital and media platforms. How is it possible then that in an era when social media was expected to give everyone an equal voice, so many continue to feel voiceless?

To be deprived of a voice means to be deprived of agency over our own lives. It also means to slowly but systematically become alienated from our own journeys, struggles and inner transformations, and begin to view even our most subjective experiences as though through someone else's eyes, an external gaze. 'There is no greater agony than bearing an untold story inside you', wrote the poet, author and civil rights activist Maya Angelou. In the present circumstances, for a whole variety of reasons, a similar agony is experienced by many across the globe, East and West, North and South.

Stories bring us together, untold stories keep us apart.

We are made of stories – those that have happened, those that are still happening at this moment in time and those that are shaped purely in our imagination through words, images, dreams and an endless sense of wonder about the world around us and how it works. Unvarnished truths, innermost reflections, fragments of memory, wounds unhealed. Not to be able to tell your story, to be silenced and shut out, therefore, is to be dehumanised. It strikes at your very existence; it makes you question your sanity, the validity of your version of events. It creates a profound, and existential anxiety in us.

In losing our voice something in us dies.

*

The year I started primary school in Turkey, I had difficulty learning how to write. Part of the reason might have been due to my own introversion and my inability to adapt quickly to the new environment. But a larger part was because I was left-handed. Back then, left-handedness was socially and culturally considered to be a problem that could nevertheless be fixed with rigorous attention and discipline. Unfortunately, among those who shared this view was my classroom teacher. Every day, she would remind me, with a disappointed smile that was worse than if she'd simply yelled at me, to please stop using my 'bad hand' and switch to my 'good hand'. There was another student who seemed to be in the same boat as I was and for a while we shared a sense of camaraderie but somehow he managed to make the transition in the space of no more than a few weeks. I couldn't. If anything, I felt paralysed.

Meanwhile, with every incentive she could think of, the teacher goaded me to correct my behaviour. She promised me rewards and, when that didn't help, she resorted to patriotism and civic responsibility, and then to religion. Did I not know that when you carried the Turkish flag on every national celebration day, you had to hold your right hand above your left hand? Did I not know that God the Almighty had placed two angels on the shoulders of each human being, two diligent scribes, whose sole aim was to note down our every move and every thought? The angel on the left shoulder kept a list of all our sins, including our darkest wishes, while the angel perched on the right shoulder recorded our virtues and honourable deeds. Wasn't it clear that by choosing the left hand to write I was associating myself with the wrong angel, siding with sin?

I was an early reader. As an only child, a lonely child, I was immensely curious about books and the mysteries they held, and at home, with a bit of help from my Grandma, I had been quietly picking up the patterns of language, deciphering their codes. But now at school, holding a pencil, jotting down words into a notebook had become pure torment. If memory serves, in a classroom of about forty-five kids I must have been one of the last, if not the last, to learn how to write and earn the red velvet ribbon that the teacher would pin on the chest of every victorious student. I might never have developed the skill were it not for a singular letter in the Turkish alphabet.

It was called the soft g – a 'g' with a little squiggle on top, like this: ğ. Always it had to be preceded by a vowel, and even though it some-times lengthened the sound of the vowel, it did not have a voice of its own. Every other letter made a distinctive sound, expressed itself loud and clear, except this one. The soft g did not talk. It did not complain or articulate opinions or demand anything. With its puzzling silence and slightly distracted manners it immedi-ately stood out amid the gushing, garrulous letters. It must be a foreigner, I thought. An outsider. An alphabetical outcast. No word in my mother tongue started with it, which I found rather unfair. It was almost as if it was invisible. If you encountered it in the middle of a word, you were supposed to pretend not to have seen it. Just move on and gently skip over it. So the soft g remained mute no matter what the text or context. Yet the more attention I paid to this mystifying letter the more I came to believe that it was trying to tell me something. Perhaps it did speak after all, in its own way, but no one was interested in hearing what it was saying. And somehow my seven-year-old brain associated this unwanted letter with my unwanted left hand. They were both unpopular in the classroom, that's how it felt. Maybe they could connect.

So in the evenings I set about practising drawing out the soft g, first with my left hand, my sinful hand, just for myself, and then with my right and respectable hand, for school the next day. I made up imaginary words that, defying the rules of grammar, began with the silent letter. To this end, I introduced slight changes in existing spellings – gorilla became ğorilla, graffiti became ğraffiti. I then wrote them down, painstakingly, though I remembered to stick to the original spellings in the classroom. It worked. The teacher was pleased, I was finally making progress. Little by little, the one mute letter in the Turkish alphabet helped me to gain confidence and guided me through the rest of the writing system. In hindsight, I understand, it was me who was struggling to belong in school and I projected this sense of alienation on to an inanimate letter. But the experience, vivid and visceral as it was, taught me an important life lesson: when you feel alone don't look within, look out and look beyond for others who feel the same way, for there are always others, and if you can connect with them and with their story, you will be able to see everything in a new light.

Still today, as a novelist, I am not only drawn to stories but also to silences. My first instinct as a storyteller is to dig into 'the periphery' rather than 'the centre' and focus my attention on the marginalised, underserved, disenfranchised and censored voices. Taboos too, including political, cultural, gender taboos. There is a part of me that wants to understand, at any moment in time, where in a society the silent letters are hidden.

*

If wanting to be heard is one side of the coin, the other side is being willing to listen. The two are inextricably connected. When convinced that no one – especially those in places of power and privilege – is really paying attention to our protests and demands we will be less inclined to listen to others, particularly to people whose views differ from ours. Communication across the cultural and ideological spectrum will falter and, eventually, crumble. And when communication is broken, coexistence, inclusion and social harmony will also be damaged. In other words, if perpetuated and made routine, the feeling of being systematically unheard will slowly, gradually, seal our ears, and then seal our hearts. In retracting our willingness to listen to others, we ensure that they, too, feel unheard. And the cycle continues, worsening every time it revolves.

The moment we stop listening to diverse opinions is also when we stop learning. Because the truth is we don't learn much from sameness and monotony. We usually learn from differences.

In life most of what we have come to understand throughout the years we have acquired by interacting with dissimilar, and often challenging views, and by encountering information, criticism and knowledge hitherto unfamiliar to us, and then processing these internally by growing insight from seeds of discussions, readings and observations.

The thing about groupthink or social media bubbles is that they aggressively feed and amplify repetition. And repetition, however familiar and comforting, will never challenge us mentally, emotionally or behaviourally.

Echoes simply reiterate what has already been said at some point in time, long gone. Like dead stars, they might seem to have a presence from a distance, but in truth, they are completely devoid of life and light. Echo chambers, therefore, severely limit the breadth and depth of the views we subject ourselves to, they ration knowledge. And, at the same time, they limit wisdom: wisdom, which connects the mind and the heart, activates emotional intelligence, expands empathy and understanding, allows us to reach beyond the lonely confines of our own minds and engage with the rest of humanity, to listen to them and learn from them. To leave one echo chamber for another is no solution either. We must strive to become intellectual nomads, keep moving, keep learning, resist confining ourselves in any cultural or mental ghetto, and spend more time not in select centres but at the margins, which is where real change always comes from.

If all my friends and acquaintances think like me, vote like me, speak like me, if I only read the kind of books, newspapers and magazines that are in line with what I have read before, if I only follow online sites that sympathise with my preconceived verdicts, if I only watch videos or programmes that essentially validate my worldview, and if nearly all of my information comes from the same limited sources, day in, day out, it means that, deep within, I want to be surrounded with my mirror image 24/7. That is not only a suffocatingly claustrophobic setting, it is also a profoundly narcissistic existence.

But here's the thing: sometimes narcissism is not merely an individual trait, it is a collective one. The shared illusion that we are the centre of the world. This notion was examined in detail by various thinkers in the last century, especially Theodor Adorno and Erich Fromm. What these writers had in common was that they had witnessed, first hand, the rise of nationalism, jingoism, xenophobia and totalitarianism. Their warnings are apposite today. Central to group narcissism is an inflated belief in the clear-cut distinctiveness and indisputable greatness of 'us' as opposed to 'them'. One unsurprising consequence of this conviction is an enduring resentment towards others. If I am convinced that my tribe is far better and worth more, I will first doubt, and then denigrate anyone who refuses to recognise our superiority.

In a world that is profoundly complex and challenging, group narcissism has become a compensation for our personal frustrations, flaws and failures. But above all, it provides a counterbalance to two troubling feelings: disillusionment and bewilderment.

DISILLUSIONMENT AND BEWILDERMENT

DISILLUSIONMENT IS WIDESPREAD and that should not come as a surprise. After all, the system – from inefficient global institutions to frayed domestic politics, from big tech companies holding monopoly power to the widening gap between urban and rural areas or between the uber-rich and the poor – is broken and we haven't found a way to fix it – yet. Trust is eroding. Never were so many big promises made to so many for so long, only to have delivered so little in the end. For decades, we have been told that we voters knew best, we consumers were always right, we the citizens deserved the worthiest services, while thanks to information technologies and commercial partnerships, other nations, too, would soon adopt our ways and through advances in biotech we would soon get to live for more than a hundred years. Even if we ran into snags along the way it would not cause us to lose momentum since history was on our side. In reality, though, people were let down, again and again. If this was progress, they felt like its spectators, not beneficiaries. Increasingly, and painfully, they were made to feel insignificant, irrelevant. And now we all stand and stare at a political system that churns out slogans like advertising copy, at a financial market that is motivated only by greed and profit, at the recent events that don't move in the linear progressive way expected, realising that underneath the polished veneer of rhetoric that we have been sold, there is – and always was – hollowness. No wonder, then, that we are deeply disillusioned.

Equally, as AI technology and machine

learning grow more sophisticated and more ubiquitous, not waiting for human cognition to catch up, and the chasm between 'high skilled' and 'low skilled' workers deepens and jobs continue to disappear, we remain bewildered. We don't quite understand how the internet works but we don't want to say that aloud because everyone else seems to be okay with that, so we must accept it too. As citizens we do vote regularly, yet we don't remember ever casting a vote as digital citizens. More and more it feels that, when it comes to digital technologies, all the decisions are taken without us and despite us. As one recent study put it, 'While there is a general awareness of surveillance, the uncertainty about how and why data is collected indicates that it happens without much public interrogation.'* We are confused – but confusion has now become a way of life.

Whichever way you look at it, this is a

---

* *Digital Citizenship in a Datafied Society*, Hintz, Dencik, Wahl-Jorgensen, 2018.

threshold moment. An inbetween-dom. A perplexing interval between a prolonged end and an unknown beginning. Antonio Gramsci, the Italian intellectual and political thinker arrested by Mussolini, wrote in his prison cell, 'the crisis consists precisely in the fact that the old is dying and the new cannot be born; in this interregnum a great variety of morbid symptoms appear.'

'Morbid', in the sense Gramsci uses it, means 'related to disease'; and we, too, find ourselves falling ill due to the state of uncertainty we are surrounded with – betwixt and between,* neither capable of letting go of the old order

---

* This particular phrase in my mind is always associated with the writings and sagacious warnings of the eighteenth-century writer and thinker, Mary Wollstonecraft, who described the social position of many women, including herself, 'as something betwixt and between', desperately wanting women to move beyond the confines of the limbo they were pushed into. (See: *Betwixt and Between: The Biographies of Mary Wollstonecraft*, Brenda Ayres, Anthem Press, 2017).

that made us increasingly unhappy nor capable of building a new world with solutions from lessons learned. We are exhausted by anxiety, consumed with anger, our minds and defences all too often overwhelmed.

Elderly Turkish and Kurdish women in Anatolia say 'beware of thresholds'. Because they see such a point of transition as the domain of the *djinn*, creatures made of smokeless fire, famous for their fickleness. I am interested in oral traditions and I find it intriguing that in that unwritten culture a threshold is regarded as the domain of elusiveness, obscurity, precariousness. To employ the same metaphor, it is frightening to suddenly find ourselves in a zone of unpredictability. But if there is one thing that is even more frightening, it is to find ourselves here all alone. To be part of a collective feels more anchored, less anxiety-inducing. This is what Erich Fromm highlighted when he explained how an individual, after being afflicted with insecurity and vulnerability, aspires to gain a new sense of safety and self-worth by equating himself/herself with a large body of people. 'He is nothing – but if he can identify with his nation, or can transfer his personal narcissism to the nation, then he is everything.'

According to Fromm, collective narcissism at times cloaked itself in nationalism. At other times, it camouflaged as religious narcissism, when believers doggedly held the conviction that members of their faith were dearer to God and far more deserving of paradise and more virtuous than others simply by being born into it. Depending on place and time, narcissism could acquire other forms of collective identification. In each case, 'the individual satisfies his own narcissism by belonging to and identifying himself with the group. Not he the nobody is great, but he the member of the most wonderful group on earth.'

Today, social media and digital communication have both accelerated and heightened group narcissism. Stuck in our whispering galleries we have become bad listeners and even worse learners. Whether in public or digital spaces nuanced debates are not welcome any more. Instead there are clashing certainties. Media panels often exacerbate dualities. On our television screens or YouTube channels almost every day we watch people from opposite camps, talking and shouting over each other. They are not there to listen and they are not there to learn. They are there to make a point, and to harangue and fulminate. Likewise, far too often, we viewers are not tuning in with the aim of discovering anything new either – ordinarily we want to see 'our guy' beat 'their guy'.

Meanwhile, the algorithms pick our preferences so that the next day, and the day after, they can feed us more of the same, albeit at the same time magnifying and intensifying the messages little by little. If, for instance, I have anti-Semitic or Islamophobic or misogynist or homophobic tendencies to begin with, the algorithms keep showing me more content in that vein, steadily convincing me that my suspicions are vindicated, that Jews or Muslims or women or homosexuals are the source of all ills. The more I follow such material the more knowledgeable and up-to-date I assume myself to be. I continue gathering 'evidence', scoring points in polemical debates with make-believe enemies inside my head. Have you noticed that people who are obsessed with conspiracy theories and take a certain satisfaction in diatribes and monologues, tend to know a remarkable amount about the subject that possesses them, most of it either pure misinformation or information filtered to suit their initial prejudices?

Feeling systematically unheard, unsupported and unappreciated can make me painfully resentful, and abiding resentment will probably turn me into a reluctant listener. If and when I am a reluctant listener, I will also become a poor learner. I will interact less and less with theories and opinions that do not agree with mine. And there will come a point when I will simply stop talking to people who are different from me. Why should I even trust them?

When coexistence is undermined in this way societies become extremely polarised and bitterly politicised, ever wary of the 'other side and their intentions'. Democracy, which is essentially about compromise and negotiation, conflict resolution and pluralism, a system of checks and balances, suffers from this constant tension and escalating antagonism.

In badly fractured societies that have lost their appreciation of diversity and their regard for pluralism, opponents will be seen as enemies, politics will become replete with martial metaphors and anyone who thinks and speaks differently will be labelled as a 'traitor'.

It is not a coincidence that all across the world authoritarian demagogues go to great lengths to incite and inflame polarisation. They know they will benefit from it. They love it when there is more division, friction, mutual exclusion. They love it when the river between 'us' and 'them' overflows its banks and drives us apart, so that we can no longer see or hear each other above the roaring torrent. The swirling waters that submerge our individual voices and personal stories is music to the ears of political incendiaries. The less that people from different backgrounds can communicate and empathise with each other, the smaller our appreciation of our common humanity, the less egalitarian and inclusive our shared spaces, the more satisfied the demagogue.

Are you one of us or are you one of them?

Are you an insider or are you an outsider?

The way such questions keep appearing in our political discourses and social practices, often insinuated rather than asked openly, though no less forceful, concerns me profoundly, perhaps because all my life I have felt like both an insider and an outsider.

*

I was born in one country (France), raised in a different one (Turkey), spent a considerable part of my early youth in others (Spain and the US), and today, I am the citizen of another country, which I call my home, my adopted land (the UK). But the place where I have passed most of my life, both as a child and as an adult, is actually elsewhere – it is Storyland. And in that enchanted realm where the sky changes colours as in a mood ring and everything speaks in its own voice, whether a pebble or a mountain, in that varied and vast terrain there are no borders, no passports or police, no barbed wire fences, and no need for any of these.

The question 'where are you from?' has always mattered to me, and felt deeply personal, albeit equally complicated. For a long time it was the one question I dreaded being asked.

'I am from multiple places,' I wanted to be able to say in return. 'I come from many cities and cultures, plural and diverse, but I am also from the ruins and remnants of these, from the memories and forgettings, from the stories and silences.'

But even if I could offer this answer it would probably fail to satisfy the person who had posed the question in the first place.

'Yes, but where are you really from?' they would insist.

I knew the format. Questionnaire style. You could only fit one word in that box, no more. In an age of speed, simplicity and fleeting glimpses, few people had either the time or the patience for long answers. So I would simply say 'Turkey,' and they would nod, satisfied. 'Yeah, I thought I had heard it in your accent.'

I have often wondered what resides in an accent. Is it a presence – an identity, a trajectory, a history? Or is it rather an absence – an estrangement, a withdrawal, a blank space refusing to be filled? And are we immigrants synonymous to our accents? Or are we, or can we ever aspire to be, more than that? This is not to deny that our accents are fundamentally important to who we are, and they are near and dear to our hearts. They are an inextricable trace of the paths we have travelled, the loves we have loved and never forgotten, the scars we still carry and which still hurt. But that doesn't mean we are *from* our accents.

A human being, every human being, is complicated – layers upon layers of ideas, feelings, perceptions, recollections, reactions, desires and dreams. By placing us into boxes they are denying us our own truth. By placing others into boxes we are denying them their own truth. And so it goes.

Unlike what nationalist demagogues claim, belonging is not a once-and-for-all condition, a static identity tattooed on our skin; it is a constant self-examination and dynamic revision of where we are, who we are, and where we want to be. Groups and tribes, just like communities and nations, in as much as they exist, should be imagined as complex, heterogeneous, diversified and fluid entities that continually evolve, change and adapt.

Sometimes, where you genetically or ethnically seem to fit in most is where you least belong. Sometimes you are at your loneliest among people who physically resemble you and seem to speak the same language. There are many citizens across the world today – and their number is growing – who have a hard time recognising their countries, walking like strangers in their own homelands. But how can we begin to talk about that sense of displacement when there isn't even a word in our vocabularies to describe it?

The closest word I know of is 'exile'.

*

Right from the start the pandemic was not solely a public health crisis. Or about political incompetence, lack of preparedness and delays in response – though these were blatantly present. Nor will the post-pandemic landscape be solely about economic recession, high unemployment and a fall in the standards of living.

What we are going through is also a crisis of meanings.

For far too long, in our social and political dealings, we have consulted the same old leather-bound dictionary that was for the most part compiled in the aftermath of the Cold War. So accustomed have we become to using this weighty tome as our reference that we no longer feel the need to look up rudimentary words, taking it for granted that we already know well what they mean. But now a strong wind is blowing in, turning the pages too fast. There is a burning candle next to the dictionary and before we realise it the wind tips it over.

Our dictionary is in flames. We reach out to save what we can, but many pages of entries are badly scorched. We must replace them, and that leaves us to redefine some of our fundamental concepts. Paradoxically, the simplest will be the hardest.

What is democracy?

We thought we knew what it was, but now we are not all that sure. Democracy, we have realised, is more fragile than we initially assumed. It is a delicate ecosystem of checks and balances that constantly needs to be nurtured and nourished.

What is normal?

Do we want to go back to the way things were before the pandemic? Was that really 'normal'?

What is happiness?

What are the values we should prioritise from now on: accumulation of wealth and a fat bank account, ambitious trade agreements and financial deregulation, profit-driven business models ... or health and social care, diversity and inclusion, positive human interaction with natural ecosystems, purpose-driven business models?

Any decision we make today will have long-term consequences reaching across several generations. In that case, which should demand our attention: the 'here and now' or the 'there and tomorrow'? Can we make sacrifices in our life habits for the benefit of forthcoming generations?

What is selfishness?

Do we agree to under-the-skin surveillance chips so that our governments can closely monitor citizens' health in case of another pandemic? To what degree are we willing to forsake our liberties, if any?

What is freedom – what are my rights and my duties as a citizen?

And on and on.

We assumed we had the proper definitions of all these core concepts, mostly thanks to the generations that preceded us, who had done the hard work. We surmised that we would never have to deal with 'the basics' as we were far beyond that historical stage. But now, with a half-destroyed dictionary in our hands, we need to sit down and rethink the entries.

This is a crossroads, a threshold. As we come to realise that we cannot and should not go back to how things were before the pandemic, we are confronted with two paths, of which we can choose one. On the one side stretches out nationalism, protectionism, 'my kind first' approach – already authoritarian leaders have been using the disruption as an excuse to consolidate their power, control civil society and further retreat into isolationism. On the other side extends the road towards inter-national communication and cooperation, a spirit of humanism to deal with major global challenges, from climate emergency to rising poverty, from cyber terrorism to the dark side of digital technologies. Although the choice between these paths will ultimately be shaped by economic and political factors, it is also dependent on another debate: Identity.

Who am I?

Do I have a single identity – based on nationality, ethnicity, religion, class, gender or geography? Or am I essentially a mixture of multiple belongings, cultural allegiances and diverse inheritances, back-grounds and trajectories?

How we define our identity will shape our next steps.

*

'This city will always pursue you', wrote the

Greek poet Constantine Cavafy, even when you go to another country, another shore. The city that always pursues me is Istanbul.

I am an Istanbulite in my heart, even if I no longer can travel back. My love and care for the city is profound, and I believe it is highly visible in my novels. Wherever I go Istanbul will accompany me, that's how I feel. We do not give up on the places we love just because we are physically detached from them.

Motherlands are castles made of glass. In order to leave them, you have to break something – a wall, a social convention, a cultural norm, a psychological barrier, a heart. What you have broken will haunt you. To be an emigré, therefore, means to forever bear shards of glass in your pockets. It is easy to forget they are there, light and minuscule as they are, and go on with your life, your little ambitions and important plans, but at the slightest contact the shards will remind you of their presence. They will cut you deep.

The motherlands we have walked out on resemble the oaths we have taken as children. We might not believe in them any more, we might not even think about them much, but they still tie our tongues. They are the secrets withheld, answers swallowed, hurts unspoken, old wounds opened fresh, first loves unforgotten. Adamant though we may be to abandon our motherlands, because God knows we have had enough of them, enough of their stupidities and absurdities and hostilities and cruelties, the truth is they will never abandon us. They are shadows that tag along with us to the four corners of the earth, sometimes they walk ahead of us, sometimes they fall behind, but they are never too far. That is why, even long after our migrations and relocations, if you listen carefully, you can still detect traces of our motherlands in our broken accents, half-smiles, uncomfortable silences.

So, yes, I am an Istanbulite.

But I am also deeply attached to the Balkans.

Bring me together with an author of Greek, Bulgarian, Bosnian, Albanian or Romanian background, you would be amazed to see how much we have in common. Equally, I carry many elements in my soul from the Middle East. So this time put me next to an author of Syrian, Lebanese, Jordanian, Egyptian, Israeli, Palestinian or Tunisian background. Once again, you'd be surprised to see how similar we are.

At the same time, I am a Londoner, a British citizen and I feel deeply and passionately attached to this country where I have found the freedom to write. I am European – by birth, by choice and the values that I uphold. And despite what our politicians have been telling us of late, I would like to think of myself as a citizen of the world, a citizen of this planet, a global soul.

I have multiple belongings.

'Well, that's a luxury', populists say. 'Not everyone can travel.'

True, not everyone can travel across cultures but not everyone who does is necessarily 'elite'. In the aftermath of the pandemic fewer tourists will be able to take overseas trips, fewer international students will apply, and fewer immigrant workers will be welcomed. It worries me immensely, seeing the walls rise higher and higher.

Multiple belongings are nurtured by cultural encounters but they are not only the preserve of people who travel. It is an attitude, a way of thinking, rather than the number of stamps on your passport. It is about thinking of yourself, and your fellow human beings, in more fluid terms than solid categories.

Maybe you were born and raised, educated and married, all within the circumference of the same town. Through your family stories, cultural affiliations, social preferences, political views, sports and arts connections, and so on, you still have multiple belongings.

A human being, every human being, is boundless and contains multitudes.*

There is more overlap, there is always a greater possibility of finding common ground between people of multiple belongings than between people of mutually exclusive identities. And yet, why is it that, at school, in the family, and in society, we seldom teach our children that they have multiple belongings and can dearly love both their countries and communities while at the same time remembering they are citizens of humanity.

*

I was born in France. Our first house, in Strasbourg, was a flat in a tower block. In the mornings, for about half of the year, sunlight spilled through the curtains, caressing with its long, golden fingers the frills of the sofa against

---

* From 'Song of Myself', a poem by Walt Whitman, 'I am large, I contain multitudes.'

the wall, the covers of the books spilled here and there. Always there would be visitors – immigrants, students, artists with hardly a penny to play with. They would read and discuss Althusser, Guy Debord and Jean-Paul Sartre, though less so Simone de Beauvoir – a difference I would notice only much later, in retrospect. Competing smells of cooking hovered in the air – Turkish, Lebanese, Moroccan, Algerian, Syrian, Levantine cuisine. The aroma of cigarettes, strong and pervasive *Gauloises*. Heated debates about social change and social justice were a constant within these walls. For my parents and their friends, back then, revolution was not a noun. It was a verb.

It didn't last long. Soon afterwards, my parents separated. My father stayed in France and my mother decided to go back to Turkey. For her, Turkey was motherland, for me it was a new country to discover altogether. In this state we arrived at my maternal grandmother's house in Ankara. A profoundly conservative, patriarchal neighbourhood. A two-storey sage-green house with a garden on three sides. Fruit trees – cherries, apples, pears and mulberries that stained your hands at the slightest touch. Evil eye beads on the walls, melted lead in copper pots, scattered salt in every corner. In the mornings when I got out of bed, I had to be careful where I stepped, because there might be an invisible genie sleeping on the floor. In the afternoons women from all over the neighbourhood crammed into the house, waxing their legs with homemade wax as they gossiped to their hearts' content. I couldn't believe how salacious and sexual their jokes often were. In the evenings there would be prayers sometimes, a more solemn mood, words in Arabic that I couldn't comprehend. I was fascinated by this new world that I was thrust into, a world where women were clearly not treated equally but neither were they weak or timid.

Here is a detail in our story, an important one. When she got married my mother was still a student and, making a huge mistake, she had dropped out of university, much to my grandmother's chagrin. Although my grand-mother had treasured school, at an early age she had been pulled out of her studies just because she was a girl. My mother, carried away by the idealism of the 1970s, had not seen much value in attending a 'bourgeois univer-sity' and she had quit without telling anyone. So years later, now as a young divorcee, she had no diploma, no career, no job. Women in such situations would be immediately married off, usually to someone older. And this is what the neighbours were advising us to do when Grandma intervened. She urged her daugh-ter to go back to university, finish her studies and build for herself a career. When relatives and neighbours objected to this radical idea, reminding that this was a divorced woman with a child, Grandma said, 'I will take care of my granddaughter – till the day her mother is ready.'

And so I was, until the age of ten, raised by Grandma while my mother went back to university, took extra classes, and eventually graduated with flying colours. She continued studying, learning three more languages. She then entered the exams of the Foreign Ministry. This was at a time when being a diplomat was usually regarded as a family tradition passed from fathers to sons.

The day we received the news that she had excelled* in the exams we went out to celebrate – my grandmother, my mother and I. In Ankara's only amusement park, next to an artificial lagoon around which families strolled, cracking sunflower seeds, we sat at a restaurant with an outdoor terrace. It was a time of political chaos and escalating violence – bombs exploded on the streets, workers were gunned down in front of factory gates, a constant tension and fear floated in the air. But in that fleeting moment, for once, the world felt serene. My mother, her voice slightly shaking, thanked her mother for the support she had given all these years. And in return Grandma said something that today, in our pandemic world, I find myself remembering.

'Don't thank me,' Grandma said. 'You focus on improving your daughter's life. We inherit our circumstances, we improve them for the next generation. I had little education, I wanted you to do better. Now you need to make sure your daughter has more than you had. Isn't this the natural way of the world?'

To Grandma, what she had done was not a personal sacrifice. It was the way things ought to be. She was also giving me a piece of advice, reminding me to work hard so that my children could be better educated and better off than my future self.

It is a memory that I revisit because it stands in stark contrast to what is happening across the world nowadays. In the past, generations across the world have gone through enormous hardships and tribulations, including world wars, the Great Depression and the Cold War. But principally, they have retained the conviction, that thanks to education, their children would have better opportunities. My mother and grandmother had an entrenched faith that tomorrow, almost by definition, would be brighter than yesterday. They believed that in the fullness of time, Turkey, with a greater number of citizens getting educated, would be fully democratic, secular. Trusting in progress was at the centre of their worldview. If every generation did their best and spared no effort to improve the conditions they had inherited from their parents, gradually, incrementally, the world would become a fairer place.

Today the faith that tomorrow will be better than yesterday is simply no more.

This is what the great political sociologist Zygmunt Bauman described as 'the parents' point of arrival' being imagined as 'the children's starting point – and a point with yet more roads stretching ahead, all leading upwards'. For a long time, the accepted norm was that youth would reach further, however far their parents might have reached, Bauman explained. 'Or so, they, at any rate, have been taught and indoctrinated to believe. Nothing has prepared them for the arrival of the hard, uninviting and inhospitable new world of downgrading, devaluation of earned merits, doors shown and locked, volatility of jobs and stubbornness of joblessness, transience of prospects and durability of defeats; of a new world of stillborn projects and frustrated hopes and of chances ever more conspicuous by their absence.'

Expectations are falling. Mobility, in as far as it exists, is not upward, but downward. A March 2020 Pew Research Center survey showed that the oldest of Generation Z have been particularly hard hit by the coronavirus crisis. Much more than Baby Boomers, Generation Xers or Millennials. And here is the paradox: Gen Z – also named iGen or post-millennials – are going to be the most diverse, well-educated generation yet. They are more likely to enrol in university, less likely to drop out of high school. But in this day and age, which grandmother can argue with confidence that thanks to education the next generation will have it easier?

As survey after survey indicates, young adults today are more worried than ever. They were already under mounting stress due to climate change, racism and discrimination, the cost of housing, rising debts, instability in the job market and the impact of social media. Now, the unprecedented social and economic repercussions of the pandemic are having a devastating effect on mental health in general, and women, minorities and young people are bearing the brunt of the crisis. It is important to note that young women are more likely than young men to face financial problems.*

---

* The Young Women's Trust survey found that 41 per cent of young women said 'it was a real struggle to make their cash last'. In a similar vein, The Prince's Trust youth charity showed financial pressures were 'piling up on young people' (*Guardian*, 29 September 2017). Research by Ipsos MORI and the Fawcett Society, revealed that the immediate employment impact of the crisis has been felt more strongly by women. (Ipsos Mori, 20 May 2020).

'Highly feminised' jobs – such as caring, leisure and other services, sales and customer services – also tend to be underpaid and undervalued and these will be the first ones to disappear in an economic recession. For women like my mother education meant monetary freedom and escape from ultraconservative norms and patriarchal limitations. In an era characterised by insecurity, fragility and downward mobility, when everything feels transient, what exactly does education guarantee?

ANXIETY

OURS IS THE AGE of contagious anxiety. A deep and ever deepening worry about the state of the world, and our own place in it, or placelessness. From newspaper headlines to lead stories to social media posts, there is one term that frequently appears in our daily lives: crisis. The crisis of refugees, unfolding tragically in front of our eyes, not far away. The crisis of liberal democracy. The crisis of Western civilisation. Ecological crisis and climate emergency. The crisis in our healthcare systems and communities. The crisis of homelessness, poverty, growing inequality, deeply rooted racism

... Then we talk about the crisis in specific sectors: fisheries, agriculture, manufacture, retail, tourism, hospitality ... What we don't talk about is what it does to us, to our psyches and mental wellbeing, this state of living under constant tension.

The truth is, there are plenty of negative sentiments all around and within us – anger, fear, discontent, distrust, sadness, suspicion, constant self-doubt ... but perhaps more than anything, an ongoing apprehension. An existential angst. All these emotions are very much part of our lives now. Even digital spaces have become primarily emotional spaces. The posts that go viral or the videos that are watched most widely are freighted with emotions. What is equally significant is how this creates a tendency, a habit of mind, that perpetuates itself through space and time. In a study conducted by the Institute for Social Research scholars have found that 'when exposed to less positive news, people posted less positive comments and more negative ones. When exposed to less negative posts, the opposite pattern occurred.'*

Children see their parents distressed at home, then they start feeling the same way. Parents meet in online chat groups or school gatherings and they exchange, among other things, their anxieties about the education system or the future in general. We are social creatures. We worry when we see someone else worry. We also panic if the people around us are panicking.

Seven days a week we are forced to contend with bleak feelings, though rarely do we have the time or the will to give them serious consideration. Whether on television, radio or online, we spend hours debating 'tangible and measurable factors'; we prioritise economy, stock markets and politics, seldom paying attention to something as seemingly abstract and elusive as

---

* 'Anger, Fear, and Echo Chambers: The Emotional Basis for Online Behavior', D. Wollebaek, R. Karlsen, K. Steen-Johnsen, B. Enjolras (April 2019).

'emotions'. Meanwhile, quietly, we continue to be burdened by vexatious feelings. We assume that we alone are stumbling under their weight while everyone else is unencumbered, getting on with their lives just fine. That, of course, is an illusion. A part of us knows that. But it's hard to resist the inclination to manage the downswing in our mental state on our own, and to keep a tight rein on our worries at all times. Also, we want to look strong. Emotions, we are taught to believe, make us look weak. The less we are capable of addressing negative emotions openly the longer it takes us to realise how many people are, in fact, struggling as we are, and how debilitating these silences are to our relations and interactions with others, and how, in an infinite number of indirect ways, they shape our societies.

Angst, it can be argued, resembles fear. But whereas fear tends to revolve around a threat, an opponent or an enemy, angst is far more subtle, diffused, pervasive. It is, in the words of Heidegger, about 'being-in-the-world as such'. And the world we are in right now is one that exacerbates our sense of vulnerability. It is almost as if we have no control over anything. When we look in the mirror – or into our mobile phones – it is not the rational Cartesian individual deemed to be the master of his destiny that we see. We are experiencing the loss of the self. 'The greatest hazard of all, losing one's self, can occur very quietly in the world as if it were nothing at all. No other loss occurs so quietly; any other loss – an arm, a leg, five dollars, a wife, etc. – is sure to be noticed.'*

All of this has a major impact on our mental health and wellbeing.

In a world that is ever shifting and unpredictable, I've come to believe it is totally fine not to feel fine. It is perfectly okay not to be okay. If truth be told, if from time to time you do not catch yourself overwhelmed with worry and indecision, demoralised and exhausted, or even incandescent, maybe you are not really following what is

* Soren Kierkegaard, *The Sickness Unto Death*.

going on – here, there and everywhere. We have legitimate reasons to be despondent. When nothing seems solid or stable any more, it is vital that we acknowledge the diverse and protean nature of our emotions. It follows that we should stop judging and shaming ourselves for not being the always happy and fulfilled citizens to which we are told we must aspire.

But acknowledging the dark side of emotions is only where we begin.

It cannot be where we end up.

So if our first challenge is to allow ourselves to experience, sincerely and openly, whatever mental disturbances are there, and recognise the presence of negative sentiments in our lives, the next step is to decide what to do with this recognition, how to turn it into something more constructive and health-giving.

But before that, we must address one other widespread emotion: anger.

ANGER

ANXIETY MIGHT BE DEBILITATING, melancholy too heavy a burden, but what is wrong with anger – especially with justified anger? It happens often – at literary festivals, public engagements or university events, someone in the audience, usually someone young, wants to convince me why we should all be enraged, and how rage is the progressive oil that keeps the wheels of fairness turning, a banner which we should wave proudly in the air against political grid-locks as well as economic, social and racial inequalities. I respect the sincerity of this *cri de cœur* and wholeheartedly recognise its validity.

But I equally doubt whether anger *by itself* is a guiding force and a good friend in the long run. It is not.

As I am writing these words, protests and clashes are taking place in various cities across America in reaction to the horrific murder of George Floyd. Videos are circulating all over social media in which Floyd – an unarmed and handcuffed forty-six-year-old black man – is pinned down by several police officers from the Minneapolis Police Department while another police officer kneels on his neck and presses for almost nine agonising minutes even as Floyd repeatedly begs him to stop, saying he cannot breathe. It is profoundly distressing and utterly heartbreaking to see how passersby, alarmed and frightened, request the officers to stop the cruelty, only to be ignored. Millions around the world have since watched the shocking videos. We have collectively witnessed a murder.

In John Steinbeck's *The Grapes of Wrath* there is a moment when a character describes her suffering with the following words: 'I am just pain covered with skin.' It seems to me, more and more, we are pain, and hurt, and loneliness covered with skin.

'Human suffering anywhere', as Elie Wiesel once put it, 'concerns men and women everywhere.' Once we have witnessed the suffering, the injustice, the immorality, what do we do next? Do we tell our eyes to forget what they have seen, tell our mouths to not whisper a word, tell our hearts to go numb, slowly? Or do we choose to speak up, speak out, connect, organise, mobilise and demand justice until justice is served? There are legions of young people on the streets of America and in major world cities right now, taking a stand. They have already made their choice.

'What should writers tell the young people who are outside on the streets now?' a reader asked me on social media.

But, of course, it is the other way round. It is

those young demonstrators who are telling us writers, along with everyone else, something powerful, urgent. And if we listen, amid the commotion, the shouts and the sirens, this is what they are saying: 'Why are *you* not angry?'

And we are. And I am.

It so happens that the protests in America coincide with the anniversary of the Gezi Park demonstrations that started in Istanbul in May 2013 and spread across Turkey like wildfire, after the government insisted on destroying a small, quaint park in Taksim Square, one of the last remaining green spaces in a city of concrete, to build Ottoman barracks and yet another shopping mall. Urban spaces are shared spaces. To have no regard for the opinions and demands of the people who breathe in that space is a common trait of authoritarian regimes.

Anger in the face of injustice and oppression is not only a dignified human response but often the antithesis of indifference. Anger is also the emotion with the longest memory. Poet and author Audre Lorde once gave a powerful keynote speech at the National Women's Studies Association, titled 'The Uses of Anger: Women Responding to Racism.' Lorde underlined how anger was an appropriate reaction to entrenched racism, and also emphasised that in a patriarchal culture 'most women had not developed tools for facing anger constructively.'

How can we turn our individual and collective anger into a force for good? I find the question important. We must be very careful here: anger can also easily turn repetitive, intransigent, corrosive. Equally, it can be a paralytic emotion. It's as if the intensity of it is enough to persuade the person feeling it that they've done enough – or else, it might keep you in a state of brooding and obsessing over the wrong without being able to move forward, to find a way to heal the wrong. Unless we manage to channel anger into a more productive, calmer but not necessarily less intense force, it runs the risk of becoming highly combustible and blindly destructive, burning through buildings and bridges and human connections, burning in a vicious cycle in which violence begets more violence. We cannot let that happen.

'I get angry about things, then go on and work', said the novelist, essayist, scholar Toni Morrison.

When the world is blatantly infuriating we can't keep repressing our anger. At the same time, we need to go out and connect with our fellow human beings and stand by those who are hurting; we shouldn't forget to look within, critically examine our own assumptions and hidden stereotypes, expand and soften our hearts; and as we do all that, we must go on and continue working just as others have before us.

APATHY

APATHY – SEEMINGLY TRANQUIL yet probably the most pernicious emotion. Just as the colour white is a combination of all colours, apathy is a combination of many emotions: anxiety, disillusionment, bewilderment, fatigue, resentment ... mix them fast, mix them hard and you end up with pervasive paralysis, lack of feeling, numbness.

Reading the memoirs of people who have survived the darkest chapters in human history, such as the Holocaust, genocides, civil wars, is an important learning experience. There is a vital question many survivors raise: 'How is it possible that such atrocities can happen?' The survivors demand to know, is it because the majority of human beings are evil by nature? And if that is not the case, then how do you account for systematic acts of barbarity and wickedness?

In order to be able to answer this question, which is still relevant, we must begin to understand how apathy works. Mass destruction doesn't start with concentration camps or gas chambers. It doesn't start with putting marks on neighbours' doors, just because they are 'different' – or imposing laws for minorities to carry particular signs or wear certain clothes. Discrimination always starts with words.

It starts with language.

As I am writing this a march is taking place in Hungary. A far-right crowd is gathering with racist banners and chauvinist slogans, demanding that the Romany minority leave the country they call home. In the eyes of these neo-Nazi sympathisers, the Romany are not equal humans. They are not even humans. They are 'vermin', who are 'infesting' the country.

How does the rest of society – and the world – respond to this?

Acts of barbarity can happen fast and on a large scale not when more people turn immoral or evil, not necessarily, but when enough people become numb. When we are indifferent, disconnected, atomised. Too busy with our own lives to care about others. Uninterested in and unmoved by someone else's pain. That is the most dangerous emotion – the lack of emotion.

One of the greatest paradoxes of our times is that hardliners are more passionate, engaged and involved than many moderates. When we do not engage in civic discourse and public space, we become increasingly isolated and disconnected, thereby breeding apathy.

When we become more engaged, more informed about all that is happening, however, we feel more disappointed, anxious, angry, surrounded with negative feelings in the face of current news and fast-moving events. It is too much to deal with. We crave simplicity; we retreat into ourselves, into the familiar. This is a dangerous moment because it is when the populist demagogue enters into the picture, promising to simplify things for us.

Here is one of our main challenges: How do we simultaneously remain engaged and manage to remain sane?

INFORMATION, KNOWLEDGE, WISDOM

'I SPENT A GOOD DEAL OF TIME wondering how we will seem to the people who come after us', wrote the novelist and thinker Doris Lessing. She was worried about our possible descent into barbarism, ignorance. She was equally aware that this could happen despite the amount of information percolating in our lives.

We live in an age in which there is too much information, less knowledge and even less wisdom. That ratio needs to be reversed. We definitely need less information, more knowledge, and much more wisdom.

It is a problem, the endless barrage of information – let alone, misinformation. We cannot process this much, and the truth is, we don't. In reality, we only skim through the news, scroll up and down our screens, without contemplating, and more importantly, without feeling. After a while, numbers don't mean much any more, whether it is 5,000 refugees who have died or 10,000, the difference doesn't and won't register unless we know the personal stories behind the statistics. Information flows amid our fingers like dry sand. It also gives us the illusion that we know the subject (and if we don't, we just 'google' it) when, in truth, we know so little. Paradoxically, too much information is an obstacle in front of true knowledge.

Knowledge requires reading. Books. In-depth analyses. Investigative journalism. Then there is wisdom, which connects the mind and the heart, activates emotional intelligence, expands empathy. For that we need stories and storytelling.

No doubt we are living in challenging times and there is a lot we need to deal with – individually and collectively. Yet just imagine, for a moment: a world without books, without storytelling, a world without empathy, would be a much more divided and a lonelier place to exist.

*

It wasn't that long ago that too many experts and scholars in the Western world confidently claimed that liberal democracy was the only viable option for the globe, now that all alternative political models had failed. The Berlin Wall had tumbled down, the Soviet Union had collapsed, and the spectre of the Second World War, alongside the dangerous cocktail of nationalism, authoritarianism and jingoism, seemed to have been left far behind. There was a lot of optimism in the air throughout the late 1990s and early 2000s, an unshakeable conviction that history was moving forward, moving fast, and progress was simply inevitable.

Back then the staunchest optimists were tech optimists. Many held the unwavering view that, thanks to social media and digital technologies, we would see wave after wave of democratisation across the world, generating more freedom, opportunity and fulfilment for everyone. If individuals were given enough information, so went the assumption, they would surely make the right choices – politically, socially, economically. So the best way forward was to enable and accelerate the spread of information and technology, and then just allow history to run its course. Such was the extent of this trust that, in the early days of the Arab Spring, when it looked like even the most corrupt regimes could come to an end and the entire region would be transformed in the hands of its democracy-aspiring youth, an Egyptian couple named their newborn daughter, 'Facebook'. A few months later, this time in Israel, a family named their baby 'Like'. Children born in an age of optimism and hope and change.

Citizens were supposed to be empowered and whole systems were expected to be democratised through the free flow of information and ideas. How could totalitarianism survive in the face of digital platforms? Back then, not many realised that social media was like the moon: it had a bright side, full of light and promise, and then, an unexpected dark side. The same digital platforms could contribute to the spread of misinformation, slander, hate speech, division and falsehood, and were received enthusiastically by autocratic regimes, extremists and demagogues themselves.

Fast forward to today and the reassuring optimism of the previous decades has evaporated leaving behind a hardened seed of pessimism, germinating fast. I find myself thinking about those two youngsters – Facebook in Egypt and Like in Israel – wondering what their lives are like. What kind of a region and world have we given them? Do they view the buoyancy that presided when they were born as a relic of the past, and, more importantly, are they burdened with anxiety and paralysis that comes from standing at a historical threshold, without knowing what the future holds – like most of us?

Too much optimism generated complacency and ignorance and an illusion of perpetual progress. It also led to the assumption that human rights, women's rights, minority rights and freedom of speech were values that other people in other lands had to worry about and fight for, but not the citizens of the democratic Western world, since they were beyond such passé concerns. These were stable and solid democracies, after all. The battles had been won.

In the post-pandemic world we understand better that no country is beyond such concerns. Now we are universally aware that history can go backwards, that progress is neither guaranteed nor steady. Democracy is hard to achieve, yet easy to lose; it is an interconnected system of checks and balances, conflicts, compromises and dialogues. It withers under widespread numbness, as philosopher and political theorist Hannah Arendt presciently warned when she wrote about the dangers of a 'highly atomised society'. We all need to be more engaged, more involved citizens wherever we might happen to be in the world.

A dose of pessimism is actually not necessarily a bad thing in itself. It makes the mind more alert, more cognisant of what is happening here, there and everywhere. But too much pessimism weighs the heart down, drains us of energy and motivation. It is emotionally and physically debilitating. Perhaps in an era when everything is in constant flux, in order to be more sane, we need a blend of conscious optimism and creative pessimism. In the words of Gramsci, 'the pessimism of the intellect, the optimism of the will'.

It is mostly through stories that we learn to think, perceive, feel and remember the world in a more nuanced and reflective way. As we gain a better understanding of the struggles of people from different backgrounds, and start to imagine lives beyond the one we are living, we recognise the complexity and richness of identities and the damage we do to ourselves and to others when we seek to reduce them to a single defining characteristic.

As a novelist, I believe in the transformative power of stories to bring people together, expand our cognitive horizons, and gently unlock our true potential for empathy and wisdom. In the swirl of news that surrounds us – the inequalities, the injustices, the seemingly unstoppable turning away from the path of co-existence and diversity and inclusion – it is easy to feel like the story we are living in is not the one we would have chosen. That the narrative is distorted by the events we are living through. That our version of truth and reality is trampled under the feet of others, who shout louder, who have more power. This increasing cacophony that crushes our voices can feel like a state of madness, a loss of sanity – a denial of our dignity and humanity. It is natural to seek out a collegial and congenial group who will reinforce our core values and primary goals, and bring us closer to the stories we want to hear and prioritise. That can be a good starting point but it cannot be the entire destination. Until we open our ears to the vast, the endless, the multiple belongings and multiple stories the world has for us, we will find only a false version of sanity, a hall of mirrors that reflects ourselves but never offers us a way out.

Do not be afraid of complexity.

Be afraid of people who promise an easy shortcut to simplicity.

Nor should you be afraid of emotions. Whether it is angst or anger or hurt or sadness or loneliness ... As human beings – regardless of gender, race, ethnicity, geography – we are emotional creatures, even those of us who like to pretend not to be, especially them. Analyse, understand and reflect upon where negative emotions come from, embrace them candidly, but also notice if and when they become repetitive, restrictive, ritualistic and destructive.

We have all the tools to build our societies anew, reform our ways of thinking, fix the inequalities and end the discriminations, and choose earnest wisdom over snippets of information, choose empathy over hatred, choose humanism over tribalism, yet we don't have much time or room for error while we are losing our planet, our only home. After the pandemic, we won't go back to the way things were before. And we shouldn't. *'What we call the beginning is often the end ... The end is where we start from.'**

---

* T.S. Eliot, 'Little Gidding', *The Four Quartets,* Faber and Faber, London, 1941.

WELLCOME COLLECTION is a free museum and library that aims to challenge how we think and feel about health. Inspired by the medical objects and curiosities collected by Henry Wellcome, it connects science, medicine, life and art. Wellcome Collection exhibitions, events and books explore a diverse range of subjects, including consciousness, forensic medicine, emotions, sexology, identity and death.

Wellcome Collection is part of Wellcome, a global charitable foundation that exists to improve health for everyone by helping great ideas to thrive, funding over 14,000 researchers and projects in more than 70 countries.

wellcomecollection.org